Unit 6

HOUGHTON MIFFLIN HARCOURT

School Publishers

Contents

The New Moose

by Renée St. Pierre
illustrated by Stacey Schuett

One day not too long ago, this new baby moose was born.

His moose family loved their new baby moose. He was everything a moose should be. His moose family named him Baby Boo Moose.

Baby Boo Moose knew how to walk
like a moose. He lifted one hoof up and
then another hoof up just the right way.
As Baby Boo Moose grew, his hoof steps
grew, too. When he ran with his mom, he
almost flew.

Baby Boo Moose knew how to eat his food like a moose. He knew to scoop dripping water plants up in his jaw. Then he would chew and chew and chew until those plants were goo. Baby Boo Moose never spewed out the goo.

As Baby Boo Moose grew up, he asked
his family not to call him Baby Boo.

"Please, just call me Boo," he asked,
and his family did that. Boo knew how
to be safe and stay with the moose group.
He stuck with his moose troop like glue.

Boo knew how to be a moose, but Boo
had this problem. He did not croon like a
moose. He did not bellow like a moose.

"What was that?" his family asked.
"Is that a cat? We hear it mew."

It was not a cat. It was Boo.

"You must not feel bad, Boo. You
won't mew forever," his mom said.

"You must not feel bad, Boo. You will
croon and bellow soon," his dad said.

"It can not be too soon," Boo said.

The next day at noon, Boo was
walking with his group. He felt sad
and glum. Then suddenly, Boo began
bellowing like a moose and crooning like
a moose. Boo felt like a moose at last.

Boo gazed up at the bright blue sky.
Boo was one happy moose. He knew how
to do everything a moose has to do.

Follow the Clues

by Cindy Taylor

Do you see something new? Just follow the clues and you won't go wrong.

One clue is that the new thing is blue. So it could be my blue shirt or my blue jeans. Another clue is that it has a stripe.

Do you see something new? You do! It is my new blue shirt.

ABCDEF

GHIJKLM

NOPQRST

UVWXYZ

Which letter does my name start with?
One clue is that the letter is between
J and N in the alphabet. It's tricky. The
letter could be K, L, or M.

Another clue is that the letter is just
before M. Now you know. It's L. My
name is Lou.

Can you tell how old I am?

One clue is that I am between 5 and 9 years old. A few numbers are between 5 and 9.

Another clue is that I am between 6 and 8 years old. Now you know my age. I am 7 years old this year.

Do you know which ball my team uses
when we play each day?

One clue is that the ball is round.
Wow! That's tricky. This group is filled
with round balls.

Another clue is that the ball has
patches of black. There! We use that
soccer ball.

Which stuffed animal do you think
is mine?

The first clue is that my animal is soft
and fuzzy. Well, all three animals are
soft and fuzzy.

The next clue is that my animal is not
like the other two. Yes, it's true! The dog
is mine.

Can you tell which food I like better?

One clue is that I like this food served very warm. Are you mixed up? You know I can eat crusty warm toast or warm soup.

Another clue is that I use a spoon to eat this food. Now you know. I like the soup better.

Do you know which food is one I eat every day?

One clue is that I must peel it before eating it. More than one of these foods must be peeled.

Here's another clue. The name of this food is the same as its color. You know! The food I eat every day is an orange.

Do you know which pet is mine?

The first clue is that I got my pet a
short time ago. The next clue is that my
pet needs affection and care.

This time I fooled you! Both clues fit
both pets because Kitts and Ruff are both
mine! I like clues. Do you?

Woody Woodchuck
and the Mysterious Ball

by David McCoy
illustrated by John Kanzler

Woody Woodchuck walked quickly
through his big backyard. He was not
looking where he was going, and he
suddenly stepped on something hard with
his right foot.

"What's this?" Woody Woodchuck
asked himself. Woody understood that
he held a ball in his hands, but just what
kind of ball was it?

Woody looked closely. It was dark
brown with thick, white stitches on it.
The ball had an odd, egg-like shape.

Woody had never seen anything quite
like this ball. He shook it back and forth.
He tried to think what game he could
play with it.

Woody phoned his best pal Woolly
and asked her to come over and see the
strange new ball.

"I know what this is!" Woolly cried.
"It's called a basketball." Woolly stood in
Woody Woodchuck's driveway. She tossed
the ball into a crooked hoop she saw in
Woody's yard.

Bam! The ball hit the hoop. It fell on
the grass and skidded away.

"It's not a basketball," Woody stated.

"I know," Woolly said. "It's a baseball." Woolly stood in Woody's yard and pitched the ball to him.

Woody tried hitting the ball with a big wooden stick. The ball just fell on the grass and skidded away.

"It's not a baseball," Woody stated. "We'll never get it right."

"Wait!" Woolly cried suddenly. "I know what this ball is called. It's a bowling ball!" Woolly tried rolling the egg-shaped ball up the driveway, but the ball just spun around crookedly.

"It's not a bowling ball," Woody moaned. "We'll never find out what kind of ball this is. Never!"

Woody kicked the ball away. It sailed up high into the sky and landed in Woolly's hands.

Woolly ran with the ball past Woody. Woody ran after her, but Woolly ran all the way across the backyard.

"Nice catch, Woolly!" yelled Woody's father, as he stood at his back door.

Woody asked his dad if he knew what
this ball was called.

"Yes, sir!" Mister Woodchuck exclaimed
as he took the ball. "This is a football.
Follow me, kids. Let's go to my sister's
bookstore. We can buy several books that
will teach us all we need to know about
this football."

One or More

by Vivian Morris

This car is called a model car. This
car is made of metal. This car's hood
shines with bright silver lights. This car's
wheel spokes look like silver, too. This car
is green, silver, black, and white.

This car is made of wood. You can't see the wood that well, because this car was painted. This car's hood, fenders, and roof were painted green.

This car's wheels were painted black. If you collect cars, you might buy a car like this.

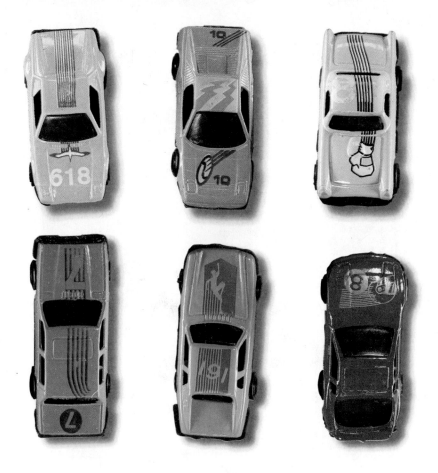

These cars are not made of wood.
These cars are made of plastic. These
cars' hoods, fenders, and roofs are all
plastic. These cars' wheels are plastic,
too. These cars' colors are not painted on.
The cars are made of red, yellow, green,
orange, and blue plastic.

This book cover has a big picture of a brown and white horse on it. The book's pages have pictures, too.

This book's pictures show different horses. This book's pictures are in color.

These books' covers have pictures on them. The books' pages have pictures, too. These books are about flowers. These books' pictures are all pictures of different flowers.

This photo is a photo of an animal. It is a tabby cat. This photo shows the cat's soft fur coat. This photo shows the cat's paws, as well as its long tail. The cat's paws are white. The cat's chest is white, too. Are its eyes yellow?

These photos show two animals, a big
cow and a duck. The animals' feet are
not the same kind of feet. The animals'
tails are different, too. The animals do
not both have beaks. Both animals do
not have teeth. Which one does?

There are three sailboats in this photo.
One sailboat's hull is red. The other two
sailboats' hulls are white. One sailboat's
sail is white and blue. Another sailboat's
sail is blue, white, and gray. The third
sailboat's sail has many colors. A boy
and his father are in that sailboat.

Howie's Big Brown Box

by Kate Pistone   illustrated by Joe Boddy

Howie paints with face paint. He
paints faces at this park. Howie likes
painting animal faces. He likes painting
stars and flowers on faces.

Howie sits in his tent at this park. He
has a big brown box. He keeps fun things
in this box.

Pam asked Howie to paint flowers on her cheeks. "I like yellow flowers best," she said.

Howie painted yellow flowers on both cheeks. "I have one more thing for you," he said as he reached into his box.

"A yellow sunflower!" Pam shouted. "It's so pretty! Thanks!"

Then, Ken and his mom came in. "I
want to look like a cat," Ken shouted.

Howie still had the yellow face paint
out. He painted Ken's face yellow.

"Now, you need just one more thing,"
Howie said. He reached into his box.

"Cool! Cat ears!" Ken shouted, and he
put them on.

As Ken left Howie's tent, Mike and
Gramps came in. "Can you make me look
like an owl?" Mike asked.

"Yes, I can," Howie said. He painted
Mike's face brown and white and his nose
yellow. Then, Howie reached into his big
brown box.

"Thanks, Howie!" Mike shouted.

Next, Jess and her dad came up to
Howie's tent. "I want a clown face,
please," she said. "I'd like a smile, not
a frown."

"One more thing," Howie said, as he
reached into his big brown box.

"Thanks, Howie!" Jess shouted. She put on her round red clown nose.

Next, Tom asked to be a mouse. Howie painted his nose pink. He painted long black stripes on his cheeks.

"I know what you need now," Howie said. He reached into his big brown box once again.

"How did you know I'd need these?"
Tom asked.

"That's my job," Howie said.

Sandy came to Howie's tent. She was
shy. Howie painted stars on her cheeks,
but Sandy did not smile.

"I know," Howie said. "Stay here while
I get something."

Howie got out a crown. He got out
some hair pins so the crown would not
start falling out of Sandy's hair. "Now,
you can be queen for the day," Howie
said. Sandy smiled a big smile. So did
her mom.

"Thanks, Howie," Sandy's mom said.

What a Surprise!

by Jefferson Redburn

There are many things to see when you step outside. Some things you see when you go out may not surprise you.

Some things you see when you go out may surprise you. A surprise happens when you see something that you don't expect to see.

A sky filled with stars might not surprise you. You know that on a clear night the sky is filled with stars.

What if you saw something long and bright shoot across the sky? Would that surprise you?

"Wow!" you might shout. "It looks like a shooting star. What is it?"

Rain falling to the ground might not surprise you. You know that rain water falls from clouds.

Now, what if you saw water spouting up out of the ground? Would that surprise you at all?

"Wow!" you might shout. "Look at that! I want to see that again."

There are things you expect to see
after a snowstorm. You might see
mounds of snow or a snowplow. What
would you think if you saw this bear?
Would it surprise you?

"Wow!" you might shout. "How did
that round snow bear get there?"

There are things you expect to see at the beach. You might see umbrellas. You might see crowds of children playing.

What if you saw a hippo like this? Would it surprise you?

"Wow!" you might shout. "It took pounds of sand to make that!"

Flowers growing in a park might not surprise you, but what if you saw a flower growing in a stone wall? Would that surprise you?

"Wow!" you might shout. "How can a flower grow in that wall?"

Seeing one balloon flying might not surprise you, but what if you saw a sky filled with many balloons? Would that surprise you?

"Wow!" you might shout. "I see more balloons than I can count."

Seeing a rainbow after a rainstorm is a nice surprise. Would seeing two rainbows amaze you?

"Wow!" you might shout. "I have never ever seen anything like that in my whole life."

While you are outside, look up and down. Look all around. Which things surprise you?

Not So Alike

by Saturnino Romay
illustrated by Karen Stormer Brooks

Shay and May happen to be the sort of
twins who look alike. Shay has long black
braids and so does May. May is tall and
so is Shay.

Shay and May have twin beds,
blankets, and pillows to sleep on at night.
Shay and May have twin desks and lamps
to use each day. Shay and May read the
same books and play the same games.

Shay and May try to dress the same
way. At night, they lay out the same
outfits for school. Shay and May have
twin pants, tops, socks, sneakers, jackets,
backpacks, and lunchboxes.

Shay and May even eat the same
things. Shay and May like muffins with
raisins and big glasses of milk each
morning. They eat the same lunch each
day, and the same dinner each night.

Last weekend, the woman next door had a big yard sale. Mom went to hunt for good deals. Shay and May hunted as well. When Shay came upon two bikes, she begged Mom to get them.

"Don't get that bike for me," said May.
"I want to get something else."

"We always get the same thing,"
explained Shay.

"Just once, can I try something
different?" asked May.

"Let's think about it," said Mom.

"May can't be different," complained
Shay. "Can she?"

"May can be different if she likes,"
said Mom.

"Can I get this basketball?" asked May
as she held it up.

"Yes!" said Mom.

Mom, May, and Shay got a good deal,
a basketball, and a bike! May and Shay
went to play at the playground. May
shot hoops, while Shay rode her bike. All
three were happy!

Corduroy and Will

by Douglas McGregor
illustrated by Valerie Sokolova

Once upon a time, a toy maker named
Will had a real dog named Corduroy.
Corduroy was a loyal pet.

Corduroy knew his master's voice and
came running each time Will called.

Each day, Corduroy followed Will
to Will's toyshop and sat with Will as
he made toys. Each night, Will and
Corduroy went home and ate a good
supper. Then Corduroy slept at the foot
of Will's bed until morning. Will and
Corduroy were never apart.

Day after day, a woman in a long
silken gown came to Will's toyshop. She
liked Will's dog. "How much is that dog?"
she asked, pointing at Corduroy.

"Corduroy is not a toy," Will replied.
"He is not for sale."

"I will pay ten times the price you
ask," she said in her firm voice. "I want
to buy that dog."

"I can not sell him," Will said.

"You must sell me that dog. I am your Queen!" she said.

Will had no choice. He sold Corduroy to Queen Noise for five gold coins. Corduroy did not want to go.

At dinnertime, Queen Noise called
Corduroy to eat. He hid under her royal
throne and Queen Noise had to eat all by
herself. Corduroy didn't sleep at the foot
of her royal bed. He slept in the hall on
the cold, hard stone.

For weeks, Corduroy annoyed Queen
Noise. When Queen Noise sat inside,
Corduroy went outside. When she went
outside, Corduroy went inside. When
she went up in her tower, Corduroy went
down in the basement.

Finally, Queen Noise took Corduroy
back to Will's toyshop.

"This dog is not loyal!" Queen Noise said to Will.

"That is because Corduroy is my dog. An old dog can't show loyalty to royalty. This puppy will be loyal to you," Will said. He handed Queen Noise a puppy that was like a small ball of fluff. It licked Queen Noise's face with joy.

"I will name this puppy Floyd! How can I thank you?" Queen Noise asked.

"Return my dog Corduroy to me. That will be all the thanks I need," Will said.

And that is just what Queen Noise did!

A Picnic Problem

by Evan Thomason

illustrated by Steven Parton

Beaver and Gopher planned a trip down the river in a rowboat. Fox had invited them for a splendid fall picnic at a lake just past an old mill. Beaver packed lunch in his wicker basket. Gopher made flasks of grape punch and tucked them under her seat.

Beaver and Gopher got in the yellow
rowboat. Beaver took the oars and began
to row. The oars groaned in the brass
oarlocks as he swung them back and
forth. How nice to row slowly and go
with the flow of the golden brown river!

Suddenly, Gopher noticed something
odd to her right on the steepest hill.

"Beaver, will you stop rowing?"
asked Gopher.

"If I stop, we will be late for Fox's
picnic," said Beaver. He kept his speed
and pace without slowing down. Gopher
frowned at Beaver.

"Please, stop this rowboat!" insisted
Gopher loudly.

Beaver saw how upset Gopher looked.
That was good reason to stop. Beaver
rowed to the riverbank and tied his yellow
rowboat to an old tree stump. Gopher
bolted out and began to scurry up the
hill. Beaver followed shortly after her.

"What is wrong? It's getting steeper
and steeper," called Beaver, trying his best
to keep up with Gopher.

"Keep going. We are almost at the
spot," said Gopher.

At last, Beaver and Gopher stopped.

Fox was stuck in the branches of a
tree, his left arm stuck this way and his
right arm stuck that way. He could not
unbutton his green coat and get free!

"Hello, hello! I'll be very grateful if
you can get me down!" called Fox, with a
wry smile. "I'll even give you money!"

"Don't be silly! Hold on!" said Gopher.
as she and Beaver gingerly plucked Fox
from the tree's clutches. Fox was free!

"Are you OK?" asked Beaver.

"I am totally fine! I was late! So, I
went up to signal you and got stuck on
my way back down," admitted Fox.

"It's a good thing Gopher saw you!"
said Beaver.

"I agree! Thanks," said Fox.

"Let us go eat!" said Gopher.

So they all went down the hill and had
a splendid fall picnic at the oxbow lake by
the old mill.

Polly Poodle

by Karen Torkelson
illustrated by Rusty Fletcher

Polly Poodle had a little shop in the
middle of town. Polly sold a little of this
and a little of that. Polly sold apples,
candles, bubble bath, basketballs, waffle
makers, maple fudge, milk bottles,
teapots, and much more.

Polly Poodle got up at six each morning and opened her shop. She went home each night at seven. Town poodles came in her shop once in a while, if they needed a little of this and a little of that. Polly made money and liked her job.

One day, not one single poodle came
into Polly's shop to get a little of this and
a little of that. So, Polly closed her shop
at noon and made noodles for lunch.
Polly placed a pot on her stove. Soon it
boiled and bubbled.

Polly made her noodles from scratch
and cut them by hand. She cooked them
by adding a little of this and a little of
that until the noodles smelled just right.
The yummy smell of noodles filled Polly's
shop and drifted into the middle of town.
Polly filled her bowl with noodles and
then sat down to lunch.

When Polly was almost finished
eating, the shop door handle wiggled,
jiggled, and clicked.

"My shop is closed," called Polly.

"What is that smell?" asked Paul
Poodle. He sniffed the air.

"Noodles," replied Polly.

"Will you sell me a bowl?" asked Paul.

Polly had noodles left in the pot. So, Polly let Paul Poodle in and sold him a big bowl of piping hot noodles.

"Those are the best noodles I have ever eaten," remarked Paul Poodle.

"Thank you," said Polly.

"I will be back for lunch another day!" said Paul Poodle.

The following day, Paul Poodle came
back with seven poodle pals. Polly made
batches of noodles with a little of this and
a little of that.

Town poodles rushed to see what
smelled so good. A line of poodles went
up the street. Polly sold oodles of noodles
to all those poodles, too!

Polly's shop grew and grew. Polly
stopped selling a little of this and a little
of that. She just sold noodles, noodles,
and nothing but noodles from that day
on. Polly Poodle's Noodle Shop was a big
hit. That made Polly happy.

Word Lists

Accompanies
The Mysterious Tadpole

The New Moose

page 1

Decodable Words
Target Skill: *Vowel diphthongs oo, ew, ue, ou*
blue, Boo, chew, croon, crooning, flew, food, glue, goo, grew, group, hoof, knew, mew, moose, new, noon, scoop, soon, spewed, too, troop, you

Words Using Previously Taught Skills
a, almost, and, another, as, asked, at, bad, bellow, bellowing, born, bright, but, call, can, cat, dad, day, did, dripping, eat, everything, family, feel, felt, forever, gazed, glum, had, happy, has, hear, him, his, in, is, it, jaw, just, last, lifted, like, mom, must, named, never, next, not, plants, please, problem, ran, right, sad, safe, sky, stay, steps, stuck, suddenly, that, the, then, this, those, until, up, walk, walking, way, we, when, will, with

High-Frequency Words
New
ago, won't

Previously Taught
baby, be, began, do, he, how, loved, me, one, out, said, should, their, to, was, water, were, what, would

81

Follow the Clues

page 9

Decodable Words

Target Skill: *Vowel diphthongs oo, ew, ue, ou*

blue, clue, clues, few, food, foods, fooled, group, Lou, new, soup, spoon, true, you

Words Using Previously Taught Skills

affection, age, all, alphabet, am, an, and, animal, animals, another, as, ball, balls, better, between, black, both, can, care, color, crusty, day, dog, each, eat, eating, filled, first, fit, follow, fuzzy, go, got, has, here's, how, I, in, is, it, it's, its, jeans, just, Kitts, know, letter, like, mine, mixed, more, must, name, needs, next, not, numbers, old, or, orange, other, patches, peel, peeled, pet, pets, play, Ruff, same, see, served, shirt, short, so, soccer, soft, something, start, stripe, stuffed, team, tell, than, that, that's, these, thing, think, this, three, time, toast, tricky, up, use, uses, we, well, when, which, with, wrong, year, years, yes

High-Frequency Words

New

ago, every, won't

Previously Taught

a, are, be, because, before, could, do, does, good, my, now, of, one, round, the, there, to, two, very, warm

Woody Woodchuck and the Mysterious Ball

page 17

Decodable Words

Target Skill: *Vowel diphthong oo as in book*

books, bookstore, crooked, crookedly, foot, football, looked, looking, shook, stood, took, understood, Woodchuck, Woodchuck's, wooden, Woody, Woody's, Woolly, Woolly's

Words Using Previously Taught Skills

across, after, all, an, and, anything, as, asked, at, away, back, backyard, ball, barn, baseball, basketball, best, big, bowling, but, can, catch, closely, cried, dad, dark, driveway, egg-like, egg-shaped, exclaimed, fell, find, follow, forth, game, get, go, going, grass, had, hands, hard, held, her, hick, high, him, himself, his, hit, hitting, hoop, I, if, in, is, it, it's, just, kicked, kids, kind, knew, know, landed, let's, like, Mister, moaned, my, need, never, new, nice, not, odd, on, over, pal, past, phoned, pitched, play, quickly, quite, ran, right, rolling, sailed, saw, see, seen, several, shape, sir, sister's, skidded, sky, spun, stated, stepped, stick, stitches, strange, suddenly, teach, that, think, this, tossed, tried, up, us, wait, walked, way, we, we'll, white, will, with, yard, yelled, yes

High-Frequency Words

New

buy, called, father

Previously Taught

a, about, around, brown, come, could, door, he, into, me, of, out, said, she, something, the, through, to, was, what, what's, where

One or More

Decodable Words

Target Skill: *Possessives, singular and plural*
animals', book's, books', car's, cars', cat's, sailboat's, sailboats'

Target Skill: *Vowel diphthong oo as in book*
book, books, hood, hoods, wood

Words Using Previously Taught Skills

all, an, and, animal, animals, are, as, beaks, big, black, blue, both, bright, can't, car, cars, cat, coat, collect, color, colors, cover, covers, cow, different, duck, face, feet, fenders, flowers, fur, gray, green, has, his, horse, horses, hull, hulls, if, in, is, it, its, kind, lights, like, long, made, metal, might, model, not, on, orange, pages, painted, paws, photo, photos, picture, pictures, plastic, red, roof, roofs, sail, sailboat, sailboats, same, see, shines, show, shows, silver, soft, spokes, tabby, tail, tails, teeth, that, them, these, third, this, three, too, well, wheel, wheels, which, white, with, yellow

High-Frequency Words

New
buy, called, father

Previously Taught
a, about, another, because, boy, brown, do, does, flower, have, many, of, one, other, the, there, two, was, were, you

Howie's Big Brown Box

page 33

Decodable Words
Target Skill: *Vowel diphthongs ow, ou*
brown, clown, crown, flowers, frown,
how, Howie, Howie's, mouse, now,
out, owl, round, shouted, sunflower

Words Using Previously Taught Skills
an, and, animal, as, asked, at, be, best,
big, black, both, box, but, came, can,
cat, cheeks, cool, dad, day, did, ears,
face, faces, for, fun, get, got, Gramps,
hair, has, he, her, here, his, I, I'd, in, it's,
Jess, job, just, keeps, Ken, Ken's, know,
left, like, likes, long, look, make, me,
Mike, Mike's, mom, more, my, need,
next, nose, not, on, paint, painted,
painting, paints, Pam, park, pink, pins,
please, queen, reached, red, Sandy,
Sandy's, she, shy, sits, smile, smiled,
so, stars, start, stay, stripes, tent,
thanks, that's, them, then, these,
thing, things, this, Tom, up, white,
with, yellow, yes, you

High-Frequency Words
New
falling, want, while

Previously Taught
a, again, have, into, of,
once, one, pretty, put, said,
some, something, the, to,
was, what, would

What a Surprise!

page 41

Decodable Words
Target Skill: *Vowel diphthongs ow, ou*
around, clouds, count, crowds, down,
flower, flowers, ground, how, mounds,
now, out, outside, pounds, round,
shout, snowplow, spouting, wow

Words Using Previously Taught Skills
across, after, all, amaze, and, anything,
at, balloon, balloons, beach, bright, but,
can, children, clear, did, don't, ever,
expect, falls, filled, flying, get, go, grow,
growing, happens, hippo, I, if, in, is, it,
know, life, like, long, look, looks, make,
many, may, might, more, my, never,
nice, night, not, on, or, park, playing,
rain, rainbow, rainstorm, sand, saw,
see, seeing, seen, shoot, shooting, sky,
snow, snowstorm, star, stars, step,
stone, surprise, than, that, things,
think, this, took, umbrellas, up, wall,
when, which, with, you

High-Frequency Words
New
falling, want, while

Previously Taught
a, again, are, bear, have, of,
one, some, something, the,
there, to, two, water, what,
would

Not So Alike

Decodable Words
Target Skill: *Reading longer words:
vowels /ā/, /ī/ (VCe, ai, ay, il, igh, -y
patterns in longer words)*
always, braids, complained, explained,
lay, May, night, play, playground,
raisins, Shay, way, while

Words Using Previously Taught Skills
alike, all, and, as, asked, at, backpacks,
basketball, be, beds, begged, big, bike,
bikes, black, blankets, books, came, can,
can't, day, deal, deals, desks, different,
dinner, don't, door, dress, each, eat,
even, for, games, get, glasses, good,
got, had, happen, happy, has, held, her,
hoops, hunt, hunted, I, if, is, it, jackets,
just, lamps, last, let's, like, likes, long,
look, lunch, lunchboxes, me, milk,
Mom, morning, muffins, next, on, out,
outfits, pants, pillows, read, rode, sale,
same, she, shot, sleep, sneakers, so,
socks, sort, tall, that, them, thing,
things, think, this, three, tops, try, twin,
twins, up, use, want, we, weekend,
well, went, when, with, yard, yes

High-Frequency Words
New
once, upon, woman

Previously Taught
a, about, does, else, have,
of, said, school, something,
the, they, to, two, were,
who

Corduroy and Will
page 57

Decodable Words

Target Skill: *Vowel diphthongs oi, oy*
annoyed, choice, coins, Corduroy,
Floyd, loyal, loyalty, Noise, Noise's,
pointing, royal, royalty, toy, toys,
toyshop, voice

Target Skill: *Reading longer words:
vowels /ā/, /ī/ (VCe, ai, ay, il, igh, -y
patterns in longer words)*
basement, finally, inside, maker, night,
outside, until

Words Using Previously Taught Skills

after, all, am, an, and, apart, as, ask,
asked, at, ate, back, ball, be, because,
bed, by, called, came, can, can't, cold,
day, did, didn't, dinnertime, dog, down,
each, eat, face, firm, fluff, followed, foot,
for, go, gold, golden, good, gown, had,
hall, handed, hard, he, her, herself, hid,
him, his, home, how, I, in, is, it, joy, just,
knew, licked, like, liked, long, made,
master's, me, morning, much, must,
my, name, named, need, never, no, not,
old, on, pay, pet, price, puppy, Queen,
real, replied, return, running, sale, sat,
sell, she, show, sleep, slept, small, sold,
stone, supper, ten, thank, thanks, that,
then, this, three, throne, time, times,
took, tower, under, up, want, weeks,
went, when, will, Will, Will's, with

High-Frequency Words

New
once, upon, woman

Previously Taught
a, buy, of, said, the, to, was,
were, what, you, your

A Picnic Problem

page 65

Decodable Words
Target Skill: *Reading longer words:*
vowels /a/, /i/ (VCe, o, oa, ow, ee, ea
patterns in longer words)
Beaver, followed, Gopher, noticed,
oarlocks, oxbow, rowboat, steeper,
steepest, totally

Words Using Previously Taught Skills
admitted, after, agree, all, am, an,
and, arm, as, asked, at, back, basket,
be, began, best, bolted, branches,
brass, brown, by, called, can, clutches,
coat, don't, down, eat, even, fall, fine,
flasks, flow, for, forth, Fox, Fox's, free,
frowned, get, getting, gingerly, give,
go, going, golden, good, got, grape,
grateful, green, groaned, had, he,
hello, her, hill, his, hold, how, I, I'll, if,
in, insisted, invited, is, it's, just, keep,
kept, lake, last, late, left, let, looked,
loudly, lunch, made, me, mill, my, nice,
not, oars, odd, old, on, out, packed,
past, picnic, planned, please, plucked,
punch, reason, right, river, riverbank,
row, rowed, rowing, saw, scurry, seat,
she, shortly, signal, silly, slowing,
slowly, smile, so, speed, splendid, spot,
stop, stopped, stuck, stump, suddenly,
swung, thanks, that, them, thing,
this, tied, took, tree, tree's, trip, trying,
tucked, unbutton, under, up, upset,
us, way, we, went, wicker, will, with,
without, wrong, wry, yellow

High-Frequency Words
New
almost, from, money

Previously Taught
a, are, could, me, of, said,
something, the, they, to,
very, was, what, you

Polly Poodle

page 73

Decodable Words
Target Skill: *the –le syllable*
apples, bottles, bubble, bubbled, candles, handle, jiggled, little, maple, middle, Noodle, noodles, oodles, poodle, poodles, single, waffle, while, wiggled

Target Skill: *Reading longer words: vowels /ā/, /ī/ (VCe, o, oa, ow, ee, ea patterns in longer words)*
eaten, eating, teapots

Words Using Previously Taught Skills
adding, air, all, and, asked, at, back, basketballs, batches, bath, be, best, big, boiled, bowl, but, by, called, came, clicked, closed, cooked, cut, day, down, drifted, each, filled, finished, following, for, fudge, get, good, got, grew, had, hand, happy, he, her, him, hit, home, hot, I, if, in, into, is, it, job, just, left, let, liked, line, lunch, made, makers, me, milk, more, morning, much, my, needed, night, noon, not, on, opened, pals, Paul, piping, placed, Polly, Polly's, pot, right, rushed, sat, scratch, see, sell, selling, seven, she, shop, six, smell, smelled, sniffed, so, sold, soon, stopped, stove, street, thank, that, them, then, this, those, too, town, until, up, went, when, will, with, yummy

High-Frequency Words
New
almost, from, money

Previously Taught
a, another, are, door, ever, have, nothing, of, once, one, remarked, replied, said, the, they, to, was, what, you